Baby Sleeping Trust Techniques:

Alternatives to Controlled Crying

By Rebecca Welton

Published by Spottiswoode
Publishing

Text copyright © 2013 Rebecca
Welton

<u>Acknowledgements</u>

I couldn't have written this book without the help and support of those around me: most especially, my wonderful husband. You are my inspiration and my anchor. It was your love, your laughter, and your cuddles that got us through our dark times and out the other side. Our children, Alexandra and Harry, who undoubtedly prompted me to write this book: you are truly amazing; you delight and surprise us every single day. My parents and John's, who always answered our pleas for help: thank you for keeping us sane.

I want to thank Christina Arnott for her advice and her enthusiasm for the book. The Southampton Sleep Clinic and the authors of wonderful parenting books: Elizabeth Pantley, William and Martha Sears, Carlos Gonzales, and Penelope Leach; and all those out there trying to give a bit of help and knowledge to those doing the hardest job there is.

Contents

<u>Chapter 1: Introduction</u>

"Please, I'm begging you – go to sleep!"

Sound familiar? This is what I thought several times a night. My first child, Alexandra, had never been a good sleeper, but it was my second, Harry, who turned our family life upside down. At five months, he was completely unable to settle himself. Up eight to nine times each night, the longest he would sleep was an hour and a half; he would nap for only twenty minutes at a time and took hours to fall asleep at night. You can imagine the state we were all in!

Friends were adamant that we should use either the crying-it-out or controlled-crying methods with Harry. I resisted at first, sure that he would grow out of this stage of night-waking, but it soon became clear that it was affecting our family life. John and I were exhausted, and to be honest, we were not at our best in being parents to two small and wonderful children; Alexandra was exhausted – in a house with thin walls,

9

Harry's night-waking was disturbing her – and Harry was exhausted because he wasn't getting enough sleep. All in all, we were not a happy family! So, in desperation, I tried controlled crying with Harry. He was six months old and it was a horrible experience for all of us. Harry was very distressed at being left alone. Alexandra was upset because, at just over two years old, she couldn't understand why I wasn't going in to comfort Harry, and I found it heartbreaking, listening to his cries and doing nothing to lessen them. I gave in after twenty minutes and resolved to never again leave my children to cry alone.

Quick Question!

I've heard a lot of mums talking about controlled crying or crying it out, but I'm not really sure what they mean. What do these techniques involve?

Controlled crying refers to methods that ask you to leave your babies for increasing intervals before responding to them. One example would be to place them in their cot at bedtime and then leave the room. If they cry, wait for five minutes before responding, then leave the room again. If they are still crying, wait ten minutes this time before responding. The next time, wait fifteen minutes. All subsequent times, wait fifteen minutes until you respond.

Crying it out refers to methods that ask you to not respond to your babies' cries. So you would place them in their cot at bedtime and leave the room. You would then not return until morning.

But what techniques could I use instead? I spent any spare time I could find researching other options, yet struggled to find alternatives. I felt desperate. I needed Harry to sleep, but had no idea how to help him learn this skill. After many hours of searching, I finally came up with some ideas and set about helping Harry learn how to happily settle himself.

Soon after, I set up a support group for sleep-deprived parents – the Walking Zombies Club – and I came to realise just how many families face the same problems. Like me, they did not want to use controlled crying or crying it out, yet couldn't find information on what to do instead. The parents I met wanted one resource that could provide them with a number of ideas and techniques that would help their babies to happily settle themselves to sleep, while building on the bond of trust between them and their children, rather than harming it; a book that would look at the family as a whole and address the effect a sleepless baby has on everyone in that family. So my aims in writing this book have been fourfold:

1. To gather together, in one place, the best tips and ideas to help babies sleep better and for longer;

2. To provide parents with a number of alternatives to controlled crying when helping their babies learn how to settle themselves and sleep through the night – my five Trust

Techniques that build on the bond of trust between parents and baby, rather than damage it;

3. To look at the effect a sleepless baby has on other members of the family and not only offer techniques that take this into account, but give strategies for parenting more than one child; and

4. To look at ways of coping with sleep deprivation – a must when so often parents have to live with this day in, day out.

I have drawn on research, my own experience plus that of the families I have helped, and have used a wide range of authors, from Elizabeth Pantley and Penelope Leach, to William and Martha Sears, and Carlos González. There is no 'one size fits all' in parenting, and even less so with solutions to sleep issues. What this book provides are different strategies that parents can adapt to suit their own family, ones that you can trust will not harm your baby, you, or your family. There are four Trust

13

Techniques for babies sleeping in their own cots and one for co-sleepers; each of them can be used to help your babies learn to happily settle themselves at naptime, bedtime, and throughout the night, giving your whole family a peaceful night's sleep. If you – like me – want options that always let you respond to your babies' needs, to comfort them and reassure them, and help them to sleep, then this book is for you.

Why not use controlled crying or crying it out?

Babies cry to get our attention, to tell us they are hungry, or wet, or too hot, or too cold, or in pain. It is how they communicate with us, and they trust that we will respond. Our bond with our babies is built up over time and has many different parts to it. Yet I believe that a fundamental aspect of this bond is the trust that develops from a parent always responding to a baby's cry. The controlled-crying and crying-it-out methods can damage this bond by telling the parent to stop responding. If a baby cries and gets no response, what is she learning? Only that there is no point in crying because no one will answer her. And if a baby stops crying when she wants attention or food, or is too hot or too cold, that baby has lost her ability to communicate with others. Not only that, but she may lose the trust she had in you to always respond to her and her needs.

Research has shown that if left alone to cry for prolonged periods of time, a baby experiences panic and anxiety. In doing so, a baby's brain releases a stress hormone called cortisol. If a baby routinely experiences prolonged periods of unattended crying and the anxiety this causes, this can lead to abnormally high levels of cortisol which can damage a developing baby's brain. But leaving your little one to cry alone doesn't just affect your baby. As parents, we are designed to respond to our babies' cries (you must admit it is a very effective way of getting our attention!). Research has shown that stress hormones increase in the parent, especially the mother, as soon as our babies start to cry, and these increase the longer and louder the cries go on. Parents also find that implementing these methods can be heartbreaking. We have a strong, natural instinct to comfort a crying baby. Stopping yourself from doing so can be difficult and distressing.

Finally, controlled crying and crying it out do not take into account how it will affect other members of the family. Alexandra was upset and unsettled when I tried controlled crying with Harry because if I didn't always comfort Harry when he was upset, would I always comfort her? By using controlled crying with Harry, I felt the bond of trust between Alexandra and me had been damaged – she had stopped trusting that I would always look after her.

It is easy to forget that babies have to *learn* how to go to sleep on their own. As a parent you have to teach them this skill. You wouldn't teach your children how to swim by throwing them into a pool and leaving them to work it out by themselves. Equally, you don't need to leave your baby crying alone in order for her to learn how to fall asleep.

So what is a Trust Technique?

My aim in devising these Trust Techniques was to have a selection of strategies that families can use to help their babies learn how to sleep better and for longer. Yet it was important that these techniques would not damage the bond of trust between a parent and her baby. Indeed, the techniques needed to build on Harry's strong bond with John and me. From birth, babies trust that you will always respond to their cries. The Trust Techniques use that as the basis for teaching babies how to settle to sleep. While controlled crying says you must leave your baby to cry alone for increasing periods of time, using the Trust Techniques means you always respond *immediately* to your baby's cries. This strengthens the bond of trust between you by continually demonstrating that you will always come when they call for you.

How to use this book

This book has been designed so you can dip in and out of it, and refer to it whenever you need to. The main chapters are Chapter 3: Sleeping like a Baby, and Chapter 4: The Trust Techniques. Chapter 3 contains lots of ideas and tips on how to help your baby to sleep better and for longer, while Chapter 4 details the five different Trust Techniques you can use to help your baby learn to happily settle herself at naptime, bedtime, and during the night.

Remember to stay flexible. All babies are different; what might work for your neighbour's little one will not necessarily work for your baby, so don't be afraid to tweak an idea or to try a different one if it becomes clear that what you are doing doesn't suit your family. Having said that, make sure you give each idea and technique the chance to become part of your little one's sleep-time rituals. Research has shown that it takes between five and seven days for a new routine to become established in a baby's brain. So once you start using a new idea or technique, be consistent in using it every nap and bedtime for at least a week. This will give your baby the time she needs to learn the new routine, so that she can anticipate what is going to happen and recognise the signposts that lead to sleep.

Throughout the book there are two types of information boxes: '**What worked with us**' details the ideas and strategies that worked for my family; and '**Quick Questions**' cover those questions that I have found parents tend to ask most (often by saying, "can I ask a quick question?")

<u>Chapter 2: Safe Sleeping</u>

There has been a lot of research into Sudden Infant Death Syndrome (SIDS, or cot death) so that while we still do not know what causes SIDS, we do know that there are things we, as parents, can do to reduce the risk of it.

It is recommended by the UK's Department of Health and the Foundation for the Study of Infant Deaths that babies sleep in their own cot, but share the same room as their parents for the first six months. Sharing a room is thought to be important as it enables you to respond quickly to your baby's needs.

For babies sleeping in their own cots, here are some basic guidelines to follow:

- Babies that overheat are at an increased risk of SIDS. They can overheat because either the room is too hot, or they have too much bedding or clothing on. The ideal room temperature is between 16 and 20°C. Ensure the cot is not close to a radiator.

- You should always place your baby down to sleep on her back. Remember to put her down 'feet to foot' – with her feet at the foot of the cot to stop her wriggling down under her covers.

- If your baby is under one year old, do not use a duvet, quilt, or pillow. Never use an electric blanket or hot water bottle for a baby.

Many families decide to co-sleep with their babies. Co-sleeping can be very rewarding for the whole family. Historically, co-sleeping has been the typical sleeping arrangement for parents and their children, and in many cultures it is still regarded as the ideal way of sleeping for families. If breastfeeding, mothers can find co-sleeping enables them to rest and doze during night feeds. There is also some evidence that suggests, if done safely, co-sleeping can reduce the risk of SIDS. However, the risks associated with co-sleeping can be increased if your baby was born prematurely (at thirty-seven weeks or earlier), had a low birth weight of less than 2.5kg or 5.5lbs, or has a fever or any other signs of illness. Families are also advised not to bring their baby into their bed for the first eight weeks, as statistically this is the time babies are at highest risk of cot death. You should also never co-sleep with your baby if you or your partner:

- is a smoker;

- has consumed alcohol;

- is excessively tired, to the degree that it may affect your ability to respond to your baby during the night; or

- has taken drugs, prescription or otherwise, that affect your perception, can cause drowsiness, or affect the depth of your sleep.

If you do decide to co-sleep, there are things you can do to ensure you do it safely:

1. Make sure your baby can't fall out of bed or become trapped between the mattress and the wall.

23

2. Ensure your baby does not overheat by using sheets and blankets instead of a duvet, and make sure these cannot cover her head or face.

3. Always put your baby to sleep on her back rather than her front or side.

4. Don't use a pillow – babies don't need a pillow until they are at least a year old.

5. Never fall asleep with your baby on a sofa or armchair.

Mothers who co-sleep tend to naturally sleep in a 'c' shape around their baby. This protects your baby from the pillow or the blanket covering her face. Many families do co-sleep with their babies and the most important thing is do so in the safest way possible.

Chapter 3: Sleeping like a Baby

Babies wake often, wriggle, toss and turn, snuffle, snort, and snore. All of this is normal, but it can cause problems for families when babies need our active involvement in order to drift off to sleep, and again when they wake in the night. So how do we get our babies to sleep better and for longer? I firmly believe that being able to settle themselves to sleep, resettle themselves when they wake, and sleep through the night are skills that babies need to learn. I'm sure we all know families whose children slept twelve hours a night from six weeks old, but the majority of babies don't, and this is the important bit: this is normal!

Understanding the different stages of babies' sleep

All babies are different and need different amounts of sleep. This chart gives you a *general* idea of how much sleep your baby or young child should be having:

Age	Total hours of night-time sleep
1 month	8.5-10
3 months	10-11
6 months	10-11
9 months	11-12
12 months	11-12
2 years	11-12
3 years	11
4 years	11.5
5 years	11

Babies sleep differently from adults. Adults normally have their own bedtime rituals, for example having a shower or bath, reading a book, having sex, or listening to some music. These rituals help us to relax, to get ready for sleep. In order to go to sleep, we use a sleep-association device – something, usually a pillow, that we associate with sleep. So lying down with a pillow (our sleep-association device) gives our body the sleep cues it needs to release the sleep hormone, melatonin, and this helps us go to sleep. We drift off into non-REM (Rapid Eye Movement) sleep – a deep sleep that is difficult to wake from. It is the first three to four hours of sleep, when we are in non-REM sleep, that is our 'core' sleep. This is when the majority of our restorative processes occur, so it is important that this core sleep is undisturbed. Research has shown that those who experience prolonged periods of disturbed core sleep are at a much greater risk of depression than those who regularly get unbroken core sleep. After about three hours, we begin to come out of non-REM sleep and go into a light sleep where our brain is more active. This is called REM sleep and is the stage where we dream, stir, and turn over. It is during this light sleep that we might even wake up, go to the toilet, or, if our pillow (our sleep-association device) has fallen out of bed, we'll pick it up before falling

27

back into a deeper non-REM sleep again. These cycles of light and deep sleep repeat themselves every couple of hours during the night.

Babies drift off into a light sleep, which they are easy to wake from (as anyone who has had to rock a baby to sleep will know, you learn from experience that when your baby has fallen asleep, you keep on rocking – as they wake instantly if you stop!) After ten minutes or so in this light sleep, babies enter a deep or non-REM sleep from which it is more difficult to wake. This deep sleep lasts for about an hour, after which babies tend to have a brief awakening before going back into a light sleep again. This cycle of light sleep, deep sleep, brief awakening, light sleep, deep sleep, brief awakening continues throughout the night. As you can see, a baby's sleep cycle is significantly shorter than an adult's.

It is your baby's brief awakenings that are probably the cause of your rather longer awakenings during the night! Remember that being able to settle yourself, both at bedtime and during the night, is a learned

28

skill. Some babies have no trouble picking up this skill, and are able to soothe themselves to sleep at bedtime and when they wake in the night, without a parent to help them. Others have to be helped: they need you to parent them to sleep, perhaps by feeding or rocking them, and in doing so, *you* become their sleep-association device! So when they wake in the night – and remember it is normal for babies and adults to wake several times during the night – just as you will fetch back your pillow if you wake to find it gone, they might need their sleep-association device (you) in order to fall back to sleep.

If your baby is under five months old

Babies' tummies are tiny. They are able to digest milk quickly which means they need to feed frequently – anything from every two to four hours, and during growth spurts, even more regularly! Babies this young are incapable of keeping themselves awake, so they will sleep when tired and wake up when hungry. Repeated night-waking in babies is therefore completely normal. Everyone has friends whose babies slept through the night from six weeks – I know I do! It is frustrating and leaves you wondering what it is you are doing wrong, but trust me, you are not alone. It is unrealistic to expect babies to sleep through – they are simply not designed to do so. As a species, it has been evolutionarily advantageous for babies to wake often overnight. Not only does it best facilitate their physical and mental growth, but babies who woke easily whenever they were in uncomfortable or threatening situations were the ones who were more likely to survive.

As adults, our sleep is regulated by a body clock called the circadian rhythm, which is set by our own sleep and wake routines, and our exposure to light and dark. Babies are not born with a body clock; it is something that develops from about three months of age and only settles around nine or ten months. Babies have to learn that they should be mostly awake during the day and mostly asleep at night, and this takes time. Babies under five months are going to wake often and will need feeding each time. It can be exhausting and frustrating for us parents, but it is perfectly normal for your baby! Keep in mind that this is a short phase and that they will grow out of it. There are things you can do during these night feeds to help your baby begin to learn the difference between night and day:

- Try to keep the room dark, or have only a low-wattage lamp switched on.

- Offer her a feed as soon as she wakes up – this way she won't get too upset or be too difficult to settle afterwards.

- Try to avoid changing her nappy, as this will wake her up even more and make it more difficult to settle her again.

- Try to avoid talking, but if you do, speak in a low, quiet voice.

Occasionally you could try to put her down to sleep in her cot, so she can get used to falling asleep on her own rather than in your arms, or in the car or pram. If you have older children at home who need your attention, try babywearing during the day. Babywearing allows you to settle your baby to sleep in her sling, while leaving your hands free to entertain your other children.

Quick Question!

My neighbour swears by babywearing, but I'm not really sure what it means. How do I babywear?

Babywearing simply means to carry or 'wear' your baby in a sling as you go about your usual day-to-day activities. Advantages of baby-wearing include:

1. A more intimate bond develops between mother and baby – mother's oxytocin increases from the prolonged physical contact (which can reduce the incidence of postnatal depression).

2. Babies who are carried tend to be calmer, as all their basic needs are met.

3. There is a decreased risk of flat-head syndrome (caused when babies spend an extended amount of time in a car seat or lying on their backs).

4. Babies develop earlier social skills – they are closer to people, where they can study facial expressions, and learn speech and body language.

It is important to have an appropriate sling for the age of your baby. Many areas have 'sling meets' these days, where parents can get advice on the right sling for them and rent slings for an agreed period.

If by five months your baby isn't sleeping through (defined medically as sleeping for five straight hours – though I bet that's not your idea of sleeping through!), remember you are not alone and there are things you can do to help her sleep for longer.

Babies over five months old

There can be numerous reasons why your baby is up at night or is having difficulty settling. Try to rule out these causes of night-waking:

- Teething
- Too hot or too cold
- Fever
- Stuffy nose
- Allergy to clothes, sheets, detergent, or dust mites
- Growth spurt
- Developmental leap
- Reflux (if you suspect reflux, see your doctor)
- Ear infection (if you suspect an ear infection, see your doctor)

Babies will be especially prone to disturbed sleeping patterns when they are going through periods of developmental leaps, for example when they learn to turn over, crawl, stand and walk, or when they are adjusting to solid foods. These might lead to a week or two of night-waking but should settle down. By six months, healthy babies are capable of going through the night without a feed or cuddles. If, however, your baby is finding it difficult to settle herself to sleep and/or wakes throughout the night and needs help to get back to sleep (if she is using you as her sleep-association device), here are some tips that you can use to help your baby learn to sleep better and for longer.

My Twelve Top Tips

For my family, there wasn't one magic solution that helped Harry to settle to sleep by himself and sleep uninterrupted through the night. We needed to use several different ideas to address different aspects of Harry's sleeping and napping. Your baby might just need one idea to help – perhaps she is overtired and so needs an earlier bedtime. Or, like us, you might need to address several aspects together. Below are my twelve top tips for helping your baby to sleep and nap better. They are general tips, some of which you might already be using, but all are important in helping your baby to sleep better and for longer. The settling Trust Techniques, to help your baby learn to happily fall asleep on her own, are detailed in the next chapter.

1. Routine, routine, routine

I can't emphasise enough how important a bedtime routine is. Having a routine, and following it every bedtime, tells your baby what is coming next. Babies and children love routine, and are most settled and happy when they have one. Taking babies straight from playing with mummy and daddy to be placed in their cot for bedtime is always going to be quite a shock for them. They will want more play, not sleep, and will probably be quite animated in telling you so! A bedtime routine that signposts for your baby that it will soon be time for sleep helps your baby to wind down in preparation; the sleep cues that are triggered by a familiar bedtime routine tell your baby's body to release the sleep hormone, melatonin, and this will relax her, making her sleepy and ready for bed. So having a bedtime routine is important, because these familiar rituals build up a pattern in your baby's mind, enabling her to anticipate what is coming and learn to associate the start of the routine with falling asleep at the end of it.

Make sure you have a winding down period, starting about forty-five minutes before your baby's actual bedtime. Try to have the lights dimmed during this winding down period as this helps the release of melatonin. Work out what will suit you and your little one best.

Ideas for bedtime routines

read some books

give your baby a bath

do baby massage

sing lullabies

get into nightclothes

give night-night kisses and cuddles to others in the house

milk feed

talk through curtains being closed and light being turned off

final kiss and cuddle

gently place in cot

It might help to have separate naptime and bedtime routines, so your baby comes to know the difference between a daytime nap and a proper, hopefully full, night's sleep. It doesn't need to be significantly different, just enough for your baby to differentiate between short naps taken during the day and a long sleep during the night.

I would suggest that for the first few weeks after you introduce a routine, you stay at home in order to get your baby familiar with the new rituals. Once the routines are established in your baby's brain, you can be more flexible. One advantage of having a bedtime routine is that you can still follow it when you are away from home or when you have visitors in the house, which helps prevent her becoming too unsettled (which could affect her sleep!)

2. Importance of naps

With babies, sleep breeds sleep. Naps are linked to how well a baby will sleep at night – good naps lead to good night-time sleeping and vice versa! But how do we convince our babies not only to have naps but to sleep for the right amount of time? And how do we know what the right amount of time is?

There are three simple steps for getting your baby to nap:

Step One: Always take your baby for a nap *as soon as* you see the first sign of her being tired. Signs can be as simple as an eye rub or a yawn, or can be a bit harder to spot – ear rubs, loss of interest in things around her, fussing, a glazed look, or being clumsy at routine activities. If you wait too long, she can get overtired – she effectively gets a 'second wind' and so finds it very difficult to unwind and drift off to sleep.

Step Two: Time to implement that all-important routine, so that your baby recognises the rituals that will end with a nap.

Step Three: Use a Trust Technique so your baby can learn to happily fall asleep on her own. The Trust Techniques are detailed in Chapter 4. Use the same technique that you use for bedtimes – being consistent with your chosen technique will aid your baby in learning how to settle herself, and resettle herself, without your help.

Now that your baby is asleep, how long should she nap? This chart is just to give you a *general* idea of how long your baby or young child should be napping:

Age	No. of naps	Combined length of naps (hours)
1 month	3	6-7
3 months	3	5-6
6 months	2	3-4
9 months	2	2.5-4
12 months	1-2	2-3
2 years	1	1-2
3 years	1	1-1.5
4 years	0/1	0.5-1
5 years	0	0

What worked with us

When I first found this chart, I was dismayed! There was no way Harry was having anything like the supposed 'right amount' of sleep. We were lucky if Harry would have two twenty-minute naps a day. But persistence paid off – taking him upstairs as soon as I saw he was getting tired, using a consistent naptime routine, having a settling Trust Technique, and finally using the Hoop Trick (see below) to get him to sleep longer – within a week Harry was having two naps of about an hour and a quarter each. Now that still wasn't quite enough by the chart's estimation, but it is important to remember that all babies are different and will sleep – and nap – for different lengths of time.

So what was this magic trick to make Harry sleep longer at naptimes?

The Hoop Trick

If your baby catnaps (anything less than an hour), she is not getting enough sleep to go through a complete sleep cycle. These cycles are important, as they provide enough time for her to become properly rested and are vital in aiding her learning: they allow her to consolidate her memories, processing everything she has seen, heard, and done that day. A good analogy for catnaps that I came across in my research is your mobile phone. I'm sure we've all been in the situation where we are heading out for the afternoon, but our mobile's battery is almost dead. We don't have enough time to charge it up completely, so we plug it in for a few minutes, hoping it will get enough juice to last us the afternoon. The same is true of catnaps: if your little one just catnaps, she will have taken the edge off her tiredness but, importantly, not getting *enough* sleep will impact how she develops mentally and physically.

I've called this the Hoop Trick because you do feel as though you are jumping through hoops to get them to sleep that little bit longer. The basis of the Hoop Trick is that you throw out all the rules:

- Wait outside her room around the time you expect her to wake up. We found we had a window of about thirty seconds to a minute to get to Harry once he had started to wake up – before it was too late and no amount of persuading would get him to go back to sleep!

- Once you hear sounds of your baby beginning to wake up, go straight in to her (remember you have a window of no more than one minute). Here is where you throw out all the rules – you now do *anything* that you think will get her to go back to sleep.

- So examples are: feed, rock, swing, stroke her, rub her tummy, put her in the pram and push her, drive her round in the car – *anything* that you think will work with your baby.

- Once she has gone back to sleep, if she wakes again repeat these steps until she has slept for at least an hour.

- You should find that within two weeks your baby will start to sleep longer.

The idea of the Hoop Trick is to get your baby used to sleeping longer at naptimes, so that she soon stops waking up (and needing you to help her back to sleep) after a short catnap.

What worked with us

It is usually better to be flexible and follow your baby's lead as to when they need a nap. However, with Harry we had to have a fixed routine for his daily naps. Some adults find fixed routines are essential in their lives. Others find it frustrating. I know I did! With Alexandra, we didn't have a set time each day that she would go for a nap. It was very flexible, which worked for her and for us. We simply scooped her off to bed when she seemed tired.

Harry, though, was a different story! Once we realised that he was not getting enough sleep in his two twenty-minute catnaps a day, we tried taking him for a nap whenever he looked tired and used the Hoop Trick to help him to sleep longer. This worked wonders for us, but an unforeseen consequence was the knock-on effect it had on the rest of the day. We found his naps often ran into mealtimes, and with a toddler around too, we often ended up with Alexandra and I eating first and then Harry eating later once he was up. Or Alexandra eating on her own and then, of course, I was running round trying to entertain a toddler while feeding Harry and trying to eat something myself! On top of that, we found Harry eating his tea later meant his bedtime routine kept being put back (or having teatime run straight into bedtime), which was causing him to get overtired and find it hard to settle to sleep.

The solution was to set a fixed routine for him that fit his general pattern of naps, but was tweaked enough so that he would eat with the rest of the family at mealtimes and still have an early bedtime. The best routine for him, and our family, was if Harry had a nap about two hours after he had woken up, and another one half an hour after lunch. Of course, this meant the rest of the family organising our day around these naptimes, something we found rather frustrating at times! But having already been through the changing sleeping patterns with Alexandra, John and I knew that all too soon Harry's naps would change, and this fixed routine would be short-lived.

3. Feed that daytime tummy

It is impossible to make a hungry baby go to sleep, so make sure that your baby is getting plenty of food and milk during the day, as this will ensure that she is less likely to wake from hunger during the night.

If babies feed a lot at night, it might for one of two reasons. Firstly, it may be from hunger, if they are not getting enough calories during the day. For many babies, exploring the world is much too exciting; they don't want to do anything so boring as stop and eat! Babies are curious and interested in everything. They love exploring, be it a new toy, the feel of their clothes, or the sound of their mum laughing. Your little one is having too much fun to want to stop for long enough to eat fully. And if you have other children, sometimes meals can be quite hectic, trying to get everyone fed before you are all off again to do or explore something new. The solution is to make mealtimes special quality time. Try to eat at the same time as your baby, and other children if you have them, so it is something you can enjoy together. Don't eat with television, game consoles, or computers turned on, as these can distract your baby from her food. Instead, try to make eye contact as much as possible and talk to her, perhaps about your day and what each member of the family has been up to. Your baby (and indeed all children) will love the attention and will look forward to mealtimes with their siblings and parents. If your baby is determined to play rather than eat, you can always have some finger food around her while she plays, so that she can eat on the go.

Secondly, some babies come to see night-time feeds as quality time with mum. Perhaps you have recently gone back to work and so are seeing less of your baby during the day. Or if there are other children in the house, perhaps she feels she is competing for mum's attention – apart from at night, when mum is all hers! Night feeds can become her special time with mum, so I'm sure you can imagine her reluctance to give them up. Try to give her more cuddles during the day, and if you can, set aside time to be with your baby without any of her siblings around. Some quiet time reading a book is great for this.

Quick Question!

My baby is seven months, so he is old enough to sleep through, but I think he is still hungry at night and I don't want to go cold turkey in terms

of night feeding. How do I get him to feed more during the day without cutting him off at night?

If your baby is under six months, I would suggest you offer him more milk during the day and make sure that his final bedtime drink is a full feed. Babies this young have very small tummies which need filling up every few hours. If he is easily distracted, you could try taking him away to a quiet, low-lit room for his milk-feeds. You should always make sure that TVs, computers, and game consoles are turned off as the flickering colours and noise can prove very distracting for babies. You will find that with the soft lighting and without toys and extra noise around, most babies will happily have a full feed.

If your baby is over six months, or is weaning, try to make sure he gets plenty of food as well as milk during the day – again this can be difficult with a curious baby that wants to explore rather than eat! Remember to eat with your baby as he is likely to eat more if you are sharing in the activity with him, and try taking him to a quiet room for milk-feeds. Instead of going 'cold turkey' and cutting off his milk during the night, there are two options that work: you can either reduce the number of times you feed him, or you can reduce the number of minutes that you feed him for.

To reduce the number of times you feed him: Pick two times that you are happy to feed him, for example, the first time he wakes up after 11 p.m. and again the first time he wakes up after 4 a.m. For all other times that he wakes up, use your Trust Technique to help him settle back to sleep. A great tip here is to ask someone else to help settle him between feeds (see Top Tip 12) – ideally your partner or perhaps a grandparent or friend who your baby knows and trusts. Once he is eating more during the day, you can reduce the number of times you feed him in the night.

To reduce the number of minutes that you feed him for: Tonight make a log so that you know how long he normally takes to feed. If he tends to feed for ten minutes each time, tomorrow night stop him feeding after nine minutes. The next night, stop him feeding after eight minutes and so on. Reducing the time, and therefore the amount, that your baby feeds during the night will encourage him to up his intake during the day.

4. Play with your baby in her cot

Play, read books, explore toys, stroke, cuddle, or tickle your baby in her cot for about ten minutes, two or three times a day. This lets her associate her cot with fun, loving memories. When she wakes in the night, she will know she is in a safe, happy place and might be less likely to need you there to comfort her back to sleep.

What worked with us

It took a few months before John and I realised just

how important this was. We were going through a really low point with Harry's sleep, and it was only when I thought about how tired and miserable we all were that I realised Harry's cot was a particular focal point for us. Instead of it being a warm, safe, fun place for him to be and sleep, it was a place he was put into when asleep and which, when he woke, resounded with his cries!

I knew we needed to turn the tide by making sure Harry loved his cot and found it a safe, happy place to be. So I set aside a few minutes, several times a day, to have fun with Harry in his cot. I would play games with him, tickling him, chasing him giggling round his cot till I caught him in a big hug; we would read books; or I would talk to him about the day. I wanted Harry to love his cot, to be happy spending time there, and I needed him to feel safe and secure when he woke in it in the night.

5. Prevent overtiredness

If you think your baby is overtired, and this is the reason she has trouble settling to sleep, try moving your baby's bedtime forward. By keeping them up after their ideal bedtime, babies can get overtired – often becoming distressed, fussy or cranky, or getting a 'second wind' of energy where they seem particularly active. They soon get too wound up to settle to sleep easily. Try moving your baby's bedtime forward and at the first signs of tiredness, start your bedtime routine. Don't be afraid to shorten your routine if she looks increasingly tired and you're worried she might spill over into overtiredness.

Many parents are wary of moving bedtime earlier as they fear their baby will then wake up earlier. But an early bedtime can often mean your baby will sleep better and for longer. A baby's biological clock is pre-set for an early bedtime – anything from around 6 p.m. to 7 p.m. When families work with this biological clock, rather than against it, they find their babies fall asleep more easily and stay asleep for longer.

What worked with us

We started having difficulty with Harry at Christmas. We had family staying and in the merriment of it all, his bedtime got a bit lost! By the time we did put him to bed, he couldn't settle and it took about two hours for him to fall asleep – during which he, and I, got increasingly upset. As this happened again for the next two nights, we took it as evidence that his bedtime was too early and that he just wasn't tired enough to sleep. So our solution seemed logical – put back his bedtime to even later. Over the next week, as we continued in the belief that he needed a later bedtime, Harry kept finding it difficult to wind down and fall asleep. We very quickly started to dread the evenings. Harry's cries kept Alexandra awake and, of course, Harry wasn't getting nearly enough sleep, so we were becoming a very tired and grumpy family! It was only when I discovered babies can get overtired that we had our Eureka moment! Friends were a bit sceptical, but John and I had nothing to lose by trying an early bedtime. That night we moved his bedtime forward to 6.30 p.m. Harry was asleep within ten minutes.

6. Be consistent

If your baby is having trouble settling, try to avoid taking her out of her room and back downstairs, as she will expect the same thing to happen the following night – and will protest loudly if it doesn't! It is only by being consistent night after night that your baby can learn what to expect. As a species, humans have developed far beyond our cousins in the primate world because of our capacity for learning. From a very early age, human babies learn that their behaviour can result in different actions, so young babies know that if they cry when they are hungry, their parents will feed them. It can be very confusing for your baby if you aren't consistent with your actions at nap and bedtime. For instance, if your baby protests at being placed in her cot one night, but you follow through with your Trust Technique so that she falls asleep, yet the following night you get her up and play with her some more before trying again, what is she learning? When she is placed in her cot, is she supposed to go to sleep? Or if she protests long enough, will she get more cuddles and more time to play? Only by being consistent will your baby learn that being put in her cot at the end of a bedtime or naptime routine is the time for her to go to sleep.

This tip is closely connected to Tip 1. Routine, routine, routine. Having a bedtime routine and being consistent in following it each and every night is important so that your baby can learn the steps that are taken immediately before she falls asleep. When you are consistent, she will come to recognise these steps and know that it will soon be bedtime.

Quick Question!

My baby just can't settle at naptimes or at bedtime. She screams for a good hour each time and we've no idea how to help. We've tried everything from rocking and singing to taking her downstairs to tire her out before trying again! What can we do to help her learn to sleep?

Make sure she isn't getting overtired. Take her for her naps as soon as you see signs of tiredness, and have an early bedtime. Work out a bedtime and naptime routine for her so that she has a winding-down period and can recognise that it is nearly time for sleep. Don't take her downstairs to tire her out, as she will expect the same thing to happen the next night. Instead, be consistent in using a Trust Technique (see Chapter 4) to help settle her.

7. Give your baby a special bed toy that smells of mum

Give your baby a comfort toy that she has only for milk feeds and sleeping. Ideally get two of the same toy and have mum, or the main caregiver, sleep with one (so that it will smell of her or him) and swap them over each morning. Make sure the toy is safe for your baby – no buttons or baubles that she might pull off, not too floppy, and small enough that she can hold it. A baby's sense of smell is extremely strong. A newborn can very quickly recognise her parents just by smell, and the smell of mum (or dad, if he is the main caregiver) is the most comforting smell there is. Babies feel safe and secure when surrounded by the smell of their mother. Having a toy that smells of mum may be enough to comfort her back to sleep when your baby wakes in the night, without the need for you to go in to her: the toy will become her sleep-association device rather than you.

What worked with us

We found this really helped with Harry. We got two bunnies (swapping them over each morning, so he had only one at a time). Harry loved to pick it up by its ears and cuddle it while I was giving him a milk feed and would snuggle down with it when he went into his cot to sleep. When he woke in the night, having a toy that smelt of me comforted him enough that often he could resettle himself without me having to go in to him.

8. Sleep-cue words

Every time you put your baby down to sleep, repeat the same sleep-cue words. Determine what will work best for you and your baby, for example, "sleepy-time now" or "dreams now sweetie". Sleep-cue words are important as they become part of the bedtime routine, and your baby will come to associate your sleep-cue words with falling asleep. So, in time, you should be able to settle her with just the sleep-cue words, and if she wakes in the night, sometimes it can be enough to simply say the sleep-cue words softly through the door. The great thing about sleep-cues words is that once your baby is familiar with them, anyone can use them. So dad, grandparents, child-minder, or nursery staff can say them when they put her down to sleep and she will be comforted by the familiar words and will know that it means it is time for her to sleep.

9. Soft music

Babies of all ages love music and some find it very comforting. For this reason, it can be a great way of settling a baby. Soft music tends to work best, so try lullabies, white noise, gentle rain sounds, pipe songs, ocean sounds, or whale song. If you introduce soft music as part of your bedtime routine and keep it on while your baby falls asleep, over time you should be able to simply say your sleep-cue words, put on the music, and leave the room. One of the main advantages to using soft music to help your baby to sleep is that it will mask the other sounds going on in your house. If you have a busy household, or a vocal sibling as Harry has, by putting on some soft music you can help your baby to focus on the gentle, relaxing sounds in her room, rather than the rampaging toddler downstairs! It can also help your baby to transfer from a noisy atmosphere to a gentle, calm one, more suited for sleep.

10. No nappy changes overnight

Unless your baby has pooed, or the nappy has leaked, do not change her overnight. Modern nappies are very absorbent and should be sufficient to keep her dry. Changing your little one will wake her up fully and make it harder for her to settle back to sleep when you are done.

What worked with us

I made this mistake for months! Every time Harry

woke in the night I would change his nappy. Let me repeat that: *every* time he woke, I would change his nappy. At one stage he was waking eight to ten times a night! I was worried that having a wet nappy was why he was waking so often, so I would change him in the hope that a nice, new, dry nappy would help him to sleep again. In actual fact, I was fully waking him up each time. So instead of a sleepy baby, by the time I had finished I would have an alert, grumpy baby who found it much harder to settle back to sleep.

11. Wait until you are sure they are awake

Babies make noises in their sleep, particularly as they pass through the different sleep stages. They grunt, snore, gasp, and toss and turn. They also wake often in the night. Most quickly learn how to resettle themselves with no outside help from a parent. Try giving your baby a chance to learn how to settle herself – when she makes a noise in the night, wait until you are sure she is really awake before going through to her. If she is disturbing others in your family, if you can, move other family members into rooms where they won't be so disturbed by her night noises. Remember it won't be for long. You can make it into an adventure for siblings – if Alexandra had been a little bit older, we would have had her 'camp out' in a tent in the lounge. Try not to move your baby into a different room if you can help it, as this will only unsettle her at a time when you want her to feel safe and comfortable where she sleeps.

12. Ask someone else to do the night duty

This is especially useful if you are the sole person feeding your baby, but you want to stop feeding her overnight. Whether you are breastfeeding or bottle feeding, if you normally feed her, she will associate seeing you at night with a milk feed. If you then stop giving a milk feed to resettle her at night, but go into her room (which is an important part of the Trust Techniques – showing her that you will always respond when she cries), she will get increasingly angry that you are not giving her the expected milk feed. Therefore, it can be much easier, on you and your baby, if someone else does the night duty. It is important that this person is someone that she loves and trusts, perhaps your partner, a grandparent, or a close friend, but not the person who gives her the majority of her milk feeds. When that person goes into her room to help settle her, your baby will not be expecting a night feed from him or her, so will resettle much more easily and quickly.

What worked with us

I found that Harry had come to expect a milk feed at least three or four times a night to resettle him. Once I was happy that he was asking for milk for comfort rather than hunger, I started to use our Trust Technique to help him learn to settle on his own. I soon found, though, that whenever I was in the room with Harry he would get increasingly upset –

because I had been consistent in feeding him at night, that was what he expected when he saw me. He didn't expect to be fed when he saw John though, so Harry managed to resettle himself much more quickly whenever John went in to him.

Quick Question!

My little one sleeps through but wakes each morning at 4.30 a.m. ready to play and start the day! This is way too early for me – how can I help her sleep later?

The first thing that most families try is to put their babies' bedtime back, in the hope that this will make them sleep later in the morning. Unfortunately, this rarely works and a baby that has a later bedtime but still rises early tends to be a grumpy, overtired baby. A baby's body clock, or circadian rhythm, changes considerably during the first year but with early wakers it has settled, for the time being, into a pattern that has her wake-up call too early.

What is too early?

This will really depend on your family and what you deem to be too early. For guidance, I tend to advise families that anything before 6 a.m. is still considered night-time. For any wakings before 6 a.m., resettle your baby using one of the Trust Techniques.

Is there any way to help my baby learn to sleep later?

Trying to change a baby's body clock by moving their bedtime later, in chunks of half an hour or more, rarely works. You can, however, try to adjust a baby's body clock gradually by putting back their bedtime by small amounts. Tonight try to delay your baby's bedtime by ten minutes only. Stick to this new bedtime for a couple of days, before moving it back again by a further ten minutes. Continue this pattern until you reach a bedtime and wakeup time that is more appropriate for your family. This allows your little one's body clock to gradually adjust to going to bed at a later time and will spill over into a later time waking up.

You can also place a few toys in her cot when you go to bed as this may occupy her for an extra ten or fifteen minutes in the morning before she calls for you.

<u>Chapter 4: The Trust Techniques</u>

About the Trust Techniques

If, like me, you've decided that controlled crying and crying it out are not for you and your family, where does that leave you? It left me confused, feeling alone and at a loss as to how we could all get some sleep. I trawled the Internet and various books, desperate for something that might help. Most advice I found was along the "if you don't want to do controlled crying, you just have to put up with it" variety. Not hugely helpful!

What I really wanted was a book that had a number of non-harmful sleep strategies we could try and, if needed, adjust to our specific situation. Harry had come to rely on me as his sleep-association device: I had to either feed him or pat him in order for him to fall asleep. I needed ideas for how to help him learn to happily fall asleep on his own. Most importantly, though, I wanted some techniques that would strengthen the bond of trust between me and my children. I needed both Alexandra and Harry to know and trust that I would *always* come when they cried, but that at bedtime and during the night it was time for sleep rather than time for play.

Quick Question!

How quickly can we get our baby to sleep through?

There are no quick fixes for babies struggling to settle themselves during the night. Babies need help to learn this important skill and this takes time. The different Trust Techniques have varying timeframes within which they will work. The most important thing is to make sure you pick one that suits you and your family. Give your baby plenty of time to get used to the Trust Technique (remember it takes between five and seven days for a baby to adapt to a new routine), but if you feel something isn't working or you think your baby would be more suited to a different technique, don't be afraid to change tack and try another one that will suit you and your family better.

What if you are too exhausted to try a Trust Technique?

If you are reading this, the chances are you're utterly exhausted. Just as I was, you might be eager to get started – you want to take the first steps of a journey that will end with your baby, and you, sleeping through the night. But it's important to think carefully about when to start using your Trust Technique. In order to help your baby learn to sleep better, you need to be consistent. That means using your Trust Technique to settle your baby to sleep, and then again the first time she is up in the night, and again the sixth and seventh times! Using a Trust Technique to help your baby learn how to settle herself will take longer than feeding her or rocking her back to sleep. This may mean that, for the first few days, you might get

71

even less sleep than before. Talk to your partner and other members of your family, and make sure you start using your Trust Technique when you have the energy to follow through with it. What helped me was the thought that in a month things would be different; Harry would be sleeping better and for longer, Alexandra would not have such disturbed nights, and I would be a better parent with more energy and patience. Try to think about how different your family will be and picture it every time your little one is up during the night.

If you are simply too tired to start today, don't worry – there are lots of ideas in Chapter 3. Sleeping like a Baby that can help, but won't have an impact on the amount of sleep you get, such as using sleep-cue words and having a bedtime routine. There are also tips in Chapter 7. Getting Through the Dark Times for coping with sleep deprivation.

Quick Question!

I want to start using the Waiting Game Trust Technique, but I'm so tired! I'm worried that in the middle of the night I'll just rock her, as I know that will get her back to sleep quickly. How can I get enough sleep so I can start using my Trust Technique?

It sounds obvious, but try to get as much rest and sleep as possible. Perhaps see if your partner, parents, or close friends could help out more. If you are breastfeeding, try to feed your baby lying down so that you can rest while she feeds. Forget the housework – if you have a spare moment, rest. Think of activities you can do with your baby that do not require much energy from you: perhaps reading books or exploring toys. It's not easy, but as soon as you feel up to it, you can start on the first steps to changing how much sleep you and your baby have; the first steps on a journey for you and your family that ends with your baby happily settling herself to sleep and sleeping through the night.

Below I have detailed five Trust Techniques that you can use: four for babies sleeping in their own cots and one for co-sleepers. These techniques all build upon the bond that has developed between you and your baby. There are varying amounts of crying involved in these techniques – from the Gently Does It Technique, where there should be no crying at all, through to the Peekaboo Baby Technique which does involve crying – but, importantly, in all the Trust Techniques, you never leave your baby to cry alone.

Trust Technique One: Gently Does It (no crying)

This is based on Elizabeth Pantley's excellent book, "The No-Cry Sleep Solution," and gives you a gradual progression of steps that wean your baby from using you, or the breast or bottle, as her sleep-association device. Start by keeping a diary of how your baby falls asleep:

Time of start of bedtime routine	Time baby fell asleep	What you did immediately before baby fell asleep	Comments
e.g. 6.15 p.m.	7 p.m.	Fed then rocked	Here you can record anything relevant, for instance the noise level in the house, or how bright the lights were.

This is important because it shows you exactly how your baby falls asleep and allows you to keep track of the changes you are implementing and the effect they have on your little one's sleeping.

If your baby wakes often during the night, tonight also make a **night-waking log**:

Time	How baby woke me up	How long awake	What we did	Time baby fell back to sleep	How baby fell back to sleep	How long was baby asleep for
e.g. 1:05 a.m.	Cry	20 mins.	Fed then rocked	1:25 a.m.	Rocked in my arms	3 hrs.
e.g. 2:45 a.m.	Cry	15 mins.	Fed then rocked	3:00 a.m.	Rocked in my arms	1hr 20 mins.

In the morning you can note down the following:

Time baby fell asleep

Time baby woke up (for the day)

Number of times baby woke up

Longest sleep span

Total hours of sleep

This night-waking log will give you a clear idea of what your baby is doing during the night. When you know what is happening you can start with *Step One – Sleepy but not asleep* (detailed below). When your baby is happy going to sleep with this new routine, move on to *Step Two – No pick-ups*. Work your way through the four steps, making a new night-waking log every ten days (so you can see any improvements and modify the four steps as needed). Your baby might adjust to each new step in a couple of days, or may take a week or so. These steps are just a guideline, so don't be afraid to change them to suit your family. It will take time, but keep persisting – it does work and is the gentlest way of teaching your baby how to settle herself. If your baby settles to sleep in your arms, for instance by being either fed or rocked to sleep, start with *Step One –Sleepy but not asleep*. However, if your baby settles to sleep in her cot but needs your help, for instance by being patted to sleep, start with *Step Two – No pick-ups*.

Step One – Sleepy but not asleep

- When you settle your baby to sleep and she wakes in the night, do what you usually do to get her to sleep – for instance, feed or rock her, but this time don't wait until she is fully asleep before putting her into her cot. As she is falling asleep, gently switch to a different way of comforting her. So if you are feeding her, try rocking her instead. If you normally rock her, gently place her in her cot but rub her tummy and say your sleep-cue words until she falls asleep.

- If at any time she cries, pick her up and start step one from the beginning.

- You might have to do this three or four times (or seven or eight times), but keep going.

- Once your baby is comfortable with this new routine, try switching the method of comfort a bit earlier – try changing it when she is sleepy: don't wait until she is actually falling asleep.

78

- When she is happy with this routine, move on to step two.

Step Two – No pick-ups

- When you settle your baby to sleep, gently place her in her cot and stroke her, say your sleep-cue words, play music if that soothes her, until she falls to sleep, but don't pick her up.

- If she cries, revert back to *Step One – Sleepy but not asleep.*

- Repeat each time she wakes in the night.

- Once she is used to this new routine, try not to touch her as much – instead stand by her cot, say your sleep-cue words and/or play soothing music.

- When she is happy with this, move on to step three.

Step Three – Look at me and listen to my voice

- When you settle your baby to sleep, gently place her in her cot and then stand just inside her door where she can see you. Say your sleep-cue words and if needed, play soothing music too.

- If she cries, revert to *Step Two – No pick-ups*. Repeat each time she wakes in the night.

- Once she's comfortable with this routine, try step four.

Step Four – Listen to my voice

- Now when you settle her to sleep, gently place her in her cot and then stand outside her room where she can't see you and say your sleep-cue words.

- If she cries, revert to *Step Three – Look at me and listen to my voice*. Repeat each time she wakes in the night.

These four steps allow you to gradually wean your baby from using you as her sleep-association device, while the gentle progression allows her to get used to each new step before you move onto the next one.

Quick Question!

My baby has to be fed to sleep. Every time she wakes in the night, the only way I can get her back to sleep is by feeding her. How do I get her to go to sleep without having to give her milk?

You have to stop your baby associating feeding with sleeping. The only way to do this is by not letting her fall asleep while she is feeding. You can do this gradually by using the Gently Does It Trust Technique.

Alternatively, you can stop feeding her as soon as she looks sleepy. Make sure you give her a cuddle and then gently place her in her cot. Once she is in her cot you can follow either the Waiting Game, the Walking

---

Game, or the Peekaboo Baby Techniques. This way she will always fall asleep when she is in her cot. By breaking her sleep association with feeding, you are allowing her to learn how to fall asleep without needing to be fed.

Trust Technique Two: The Waiting Game (little or no crying)

Your baby should learn how to soothe herself to sleep more quickly using the Waiting Game than by using the Gently Does It Technique. It does involve some crying, but it is important to remember that you never leave your baby crying alone. Instead you are building on the trust between you and your baby – you are showing her that you will never leave her alone when she cries, while teaching her the skills she needs to fall asleep happily on her own.

- Follow your usual nap or bedtime routine, but this time end it with you gently placing your baby in her cot.

- Stay next to the cot, but try to avoid eye contact. If she cries, repeat your sleep-cue words, play soft music, rub her tummy, or stroke her, but do not pick her up. Stay with her until she falls asleep.

- Once she is used to this new routine (it may take a few days), try to move a bit further away from her cot – perhaps an arms-length away – as soon as you have placed her in her cot. Still play music to her, but don't touch her. Stay with her until she falls asleep.

- When she is comfortable with this, move further away again, perhaps halfway between her cot and the door. Again, continue to play music if she cries, but don't touch her and try to avoid eye contact.

- Once she is happy falling asleep in this way, try to move further towards the door every few days.

- Eventually she'll be happy to be placed in her cot and for you to leave the room.

- Use this Waiting Game Trust Technique every time she wakes in the night.

If your baby is struggling to get used to you leaving the room, instead of reverting to sitting in her room, you can try sitting outside her door but where she can see you. This allows her to get used to you not being in the room when she falls asleep, but knowing that you are just outside gives her the comfort she needs to drift off to sleep.

Trust Technique Three: The Walking Game (little or no crying)

In terms of how quickly this technique will work, i.e. with you being able to place your baby in her cot and then leave the room while she happily settles herself to sleep, the Walking Game Technique is similar to the Waiting Game. It does involve some crying, but, again, it is important to remember that you never leave your to baby cry alone. Instead you are supporting the bond of trust between you and your baby by showing her that she won't be left alone when she cries, while also teaching her how to settle herself.

- Follow your normal bedtime routine, but this time end it with you gently placing your baby in her cot.

- Either stand or sit by her cot. This is your starting point. If she cries, repeat your sleep-cue words or play soft music, but do not pick her up, and try to avoid eye contact.

- After three minutes take a small step, or shuffle if you are sitting down, towards the door. Make sure your movement is slow; you are trying to avoid drawing attention to the fact that you are moving away.

- Wait a further three minutes before taking another small step. Continue making small steps towards the door every three minutes. Once you reach the door, if you need to open it in order to get out of the room, make sure you do so very slowly, a small crack every minute or so.

- Once she is used to this routine, move your starting point one step away from her cot. Continue to move the starting point towards the door, one step at a time, every few days.

- If she cries, you have two options: a) go all the way back to your starting point and repeat your sleep-cue words, but don't touch her and remember to avoid eye contact. Wait three minutes and then start again. Or b) instead of going all the way back to your starting point, make one large, obvious step towards her. Repeat your sleep-cue words and then wait there for three minutes before starting to head towards the door again.

- Use the Walking Game Trust Technique every time she wakes in the night.

- She will eventually be happy to be placed in her cot at nap and bedtime, and for you to immediately leave the room while she settles herself to sleep.

The aim of the Walking Game is to gradually retreat from your baby's room while she is sleepy, but not yet asleep. Your slow withdrawal from the room allows her to be comforted by your presence, whilst getting her used to you leaving the room at the end of the bedtime routine.

Trust Technique Four: Peekaboo Baby (crying involved!)

This Trust Technique is for babies aged six months or older because of the crying involved. Before you try this technique, you should be confident in being able to distinguish an angry cry from a distressed one. It is important to remember that with Peekaboo Baby you always *immediately* respond to your baby's cries and you never leave her to cry alone.

- Follow your normal naptime or bedtime routine, then gently place your baby in her cot, saying your sleep-cue words.

- Leave the room.

- As soon as she starts to cry, or if she continues to cry, go back to her. Briefly reassure her and then leave the room again.

- Don't touch her or pick her up.

- Remain in the room only long enough for you to get close to her and reassure her that you will keep coming back if she needs you.

What worked with us

I would measure how long to stay in Harry's room by walking the full length of his cot and back again, repeating these words: "It's alright, it's okay, sleepy-byes now."

- Don't stay away for long – if she is crying, you should go to her immediately.

- Remember that she is crying because she is angry you are not doing what she wants – to be picked up.

- If at any time your baby's cries spill over into distress, cuddle, stroke, or pat her in her cot (try not to get her out of the cot) until she calms down, then start again.

- If she wakes in the night, follow the Peekaboo Baby routine.

- The aim is to reinforce the idea that you will always respond to her cries, whilst being firm that it is sleep time not playtime.

Initially, you will probably spend most of your evening doing Peekaboo Baby, but it is unusual for it to take more than a week before your baby will happily settle by herself. You should then be able to say goodnight to your baby, place her in her cot, and leave the room without her getting upset or giving more than a protest cry at your departure.

Trust Technique Five: Playing Dumb (for co-sleepers)

Just because you co-sleep doesn't mean your baby will automatically know how to settle herself to sleep. She might still need feeding, a warm hand on her tummy, or stroking in order to settle herself when she wakes in the night. Of course when you co-sleep, the aim is the same: to help your baby learn how to settle herself without any assistance from you. Yet it is more difficult because you are right next to her. It is only natural to want to reach out a comforting hand and pat or stroke her back to sleep. But being woken up to do this several times a night takes its toll. You need to help your baby learn how to settle herself and not use you as her sleep-association device, whilst being firm that it is sleep time not playtime.

How it works:

- If you want your baby to learn to settle to sleep by herself at naptime and bedtime, use one of the first four Trust Techniques when you put her down to sleep.

- If your baby then wakes during the night, briefly stroke or pat her and say your sleep-cue words. Then *play dumb* – pretend you are asleep. Your baby will probably crawl over you, paw you, pull your hair, pat your face, explore your nose – try to put up with this and continue to play dumb.

- If she cries, say your sleep-cues words every minute, but don't show any other signs of waking up.

- Each night, gradually lengthen the time between saying your sleep-cue words.

- The first few nights it might take an hour or more before your baby goes back to sleep, but she will soon get the idea that it is sleep time, not playtime.

Each of these five Trust Techniques will help your baby learn how to happily settle herself to sleep at naptime and bedtime, and every time she wakes in the night. They offer families a choice of options for weaning their little one off using unsuitable sleep-association devices, such as your feeding them or rocking them. Remember that night-waking is normal, but by using a Trust Technique you can be confident of teaching your baby the skills needed to happily settle herself to sleep, without damaging the precious bond of trust between you.

Chapter 5: Co-Sleepers

Although the official advice in most Western countries is to not co-sleep with your baby, many families do co-sleep and wouldn't have it any other way! There are some overlooked advantages of co-sleeping: breastfeeding mums tend to get more rest if they co-sleep with their babies, as they can doze while their baby is feeding; and as long as neither partner is a smoker and they avoid drinking alcohol, taking drugs, or falling asleep with the baby on the sofa, then co-sleeping can actually reduce the risks of Sudden Infant Death Syndrome (SIDS – or cot death). Research has shown that in Asian countries where co-sleeping is the norm, the rate of SIDS is much lower than in countries such as Britain and America where sleeping apart is normal. Although researchers say there is not a definitive reason for such a difference in SIDS rates, most agree that co-sleeping is part of the reason that Asian countries experience far fewer cot deaths than Western countries. If you do decide to co-sleep with your baby, the important thing is to do so safely. See Chapter 2: Safe Sleeping for all the safety guidelines.

Many women who co-sleep also tend to breastfeed. One of my most precious memories of my children is breastfeeding them in the middle of the night: of me and either Alexandra or Harry curled up next to each other in bed, both of us drifting off to sleep again. Breastfeeding and co-sleeping, though, can cause some difficulties when your baby comes to see you as an all-night vending machine! Here are my top tips for the all-night nurser:

1. Remember to feed that daytime tummy. As I said in Tip 3 of my Twelve Top Tips, it is impossible to make a hungry baby sleep. Make sure she is getting plenty of food and milk during the day. If she is too busy exploring to stop and eat for long during the day, make sure you all sit down to eat together. Family mealtimes are great ways to interest babies and children in food, especially if you pay them lots of attention

96

while they are eating. If this still isn't enough for your curious little one, have finger food around her while she plays. If you feel she is feeding at night as it is 'special time' with mum, make sure you increase her one-on-one time with you during the day. Some quiet time with you reading books is great for this, or you could either start babywearing (see the **Quick Question** at the start of Chapter 3: Sleeping like a baby) or increase the amount of time you baby-wear during the day.

2. Use one of the Trust Techniques to help your baby learn to have another sleep-association device. If she needs to be fed to sleep, you and your breast have become her sleep-association device, and she'll need you each time she wakes in the night. Make sure you use a Trust Technique every nap and bedtime and, if you are happy that she is feeding out of habit and not out of hunger, use Trust Technique Five: Playing

Dumb each time she wakes in the night. This lets her know that night-time is for sleep, not for feeding. Make sure she is offered more food and milk during the day: although she is feeding out of habit and not hunger, she will still miss those extra calories.

3. Babies can smell milk from a very young age, so make sure you are covered up while you sleep. Some babies may also give up and go back to sleep if they can't find your breast quickly.

4. If you can, ask your partner to sleep next to her for a few nights. She will not expect to be fed from your partner during the night, so may be easier to settle.

Chapter 6: Siblings

Most baby books simply address the issue of the baby's sleep, without any thought for the rest of the family and the effect on them. This is fine if you have only the one, but what if you have another child at home? Unless your children can sleep at opposite ends of a (very big!) house, they will undoubtedly be disturbed by the baby waking in the night. Even if it doesn't wake them up fully, it can prevent them getting that much needed non-REM sleep. Alexandra would rarely wake up when Harry was up in the night, but we certainly noticed how tired she was during the day. You can minimise the effect on your other children for the first few months, when it is much more likely that your baby will be up several times, by having your new addition sleep in your room. You can co-sleep, if that is what suits your family best, or have a Moses basket or cot next to your bed.

But what happens when your baby is bigger and is in her own room or a shared room with her siblings, and still has difficulty sleeping through? Techniques such as controlled crying and crying it out fail to address how using them will affect your other children. What must be going through their minds when you leave their sibling to cry alone and unanswered? And if you don't respond when the baby cries, does this mean you won't respond when they cry? It can be very confusing and unsettling for other children in the house, and can affect the bond of trust you have with them. The Trust Techniques detailed in Chapter 4 rely on the premise that you always respond to your baby's cries. Hearing their baby sibling cry is upsetting for children, no matter how young or old, but they are always comforted to know that someone is with their baby brother or sister.

I find having more than one child to be quite a juggling act, especially when one of them found it difficult to settle to sleep on his or her own and needed more attention. Here are some tips that can help your juggling act:

- Always try to explain to your other children what is happening. Children are most often unsettled when they don't know or understand what is happening. Why is the baby crying? Why is she awake so much during the night? Why are mum and dad so tired all the time? Even young children can understand simple, basic explanations and will feel much happier knowing what is happening and why.

What worked with us

Alexandra was only nineteen months when Harry was born, but she was able to understand that babies cry when they are hungry and that they are hungry a lot! By the time Harry moved into his own room, right next to Alexandra's, she was a little over two years old and more able to understand that Harry "found it hard to sleep sometimes". When we used the Peekaboo Baby Trust Technique she was always comforted that someone was there with Harry, trying to help him to sleep.

- If you have decided to use the Peekaboo Baby Trust Technique, which does involve crying, you should consider the effect of this on your other children. No matter how old they are, explain what you are doing to help their baby brother or sister to sleep better. If possible, ask if your other children can stay with their grandparents for the first couple of days – this will enable you to concentrate on your baby, and will also mean your other children get undisturbed sleep.

- While you are feeding your baby or helping her to settle, your other children can have some special time with your partner or their grandparents. Make a big deal of this and have particular games or toys that only come out during this time. Try to ensure that the activities are reasonably quiet though (perhaps reading favourite books) so as not to distract your baby. This special time is particularly helpful if your other children are feeling jealous of the attention the baby receives.

- Have your other children help you bath the baby and get her ready for bed. Asking their help makes them feel involved, and giving lots of praise for helping builds their confidence.

- There will always be times when you are alone with your children and the baby needs a nap or to settle down for the night. If you have a young child as well as a baby, it can be quite worrying, thinking about what the older one will get up to if you have to spend time settling the baby. Try placing some quiet toys and books either in a bag just inside the baby's room, or if your child is older, outside the room or in her own room if it is near enough, and ask her to play or read while you

103

settle the baby. It can help if toys and books are 'special' ones that only come out when you are feeding or settling the baby. Remember to give her lots of praise for playing quietly and to give her plenty of attention once the baby is asleep. You might also consider giving her an instant reward, for example a sticker, for playing quietly. Stickers can be great because the child can then show it to others, such as daddy and/or friends and relatives, while you explain why they got it – for example, for playing quietly while mummy was feeding the baby. This positive reinforcement of good behaviour helps your child learn to play quietly while you are feeding and settling your baby. If your child is over three, you can use a reward system (see the **Quick Question** below). Alternatively, you can put both baby and children to bed at the same time. This allows you to concentrate on helping your baby learn to settle on her own, knowing that your other little ones are safely tucked up in bed.

Quick Question!

I have a three-and-a-half-year-old son, as well as an eight-month-old daughter. He is noisy and excited all the time! We normally find this endearing, but how can I get him to play quietly when I'm settling my daughter?

If your child is over three you can use a reward system to help him learn to play quietly while you feed and settle your baby. The aim is not to bribe your child, but to provide motivation and positive reinforcement for good behaviour. There are quite a few reward systems you can use. One example is the voucher system: on a piece of paper or cardboard, make some vouchers with a picture of the reward your son will get, so for example it might be a book of stickers, or a small toy or book, or a trip to the library or park. Show your son the vouchers and explain what he needs to do in order to get a voucher (play quietly while you are settling your daughter). Explain again each time you settle your daughter. If he plays quietly, reward him with a voucher and lots of praise. It is important that he gets the reward on the voucher within three days. If he doesn't manage to play quietly, give him lots of praise for even the smallest amount of time when he does manage to play quietly, and remind him that if he can do it for a bit longer next time, he will get a voucher.

After three consecutive days of your son getting reward vouchers each time you settle your daughter, cut the vouchers into two pieces. Now it is a voucher jigsaw and he has to collect both pieces before he gets his reward. Once he consistently gets a piece of voucher, you can cut it again, into three pieces. Don't cut the vouchers into more than three pieces, and remember to give him plenty of praise.

What worked with us

With John working shifts, there are always a few evenings a week where I put the children to bed on my own. With Alexandra so young though, I couldn't leave her unattended for the length of time it took me to get Harry settled. The way round this was for Alexandra and me to bath Harry – she loved helping out with this – and get him ready for bed. I would then pop him in his bouncy chair so he could watch me bath and dress Alexandra. Then it was a bedtime story for them both, before tucking Alexandra in bed and a final, quiet milk feed for Harry. I found this worked really well, as it took all the stress out of bedtimes – I wasn't worried about what she might be up to, or if she was feeling alone, while I was feeding and settling Harry.

Chapter 7: Getting Through the Dark Times

Having a baby that doesn't sleep, and doesn't allow you to sleep, can be physically exhausting, but it is emotionally draining too. We are all at our best when we have had enough sleep. Raising and caring for a baby can be difficult enough without the added strain of doing it when severely sleep deprived. I know because I have been through it. The days when it hurts to keep your eyes open, when all you can think about is when you might next get to rest; the days you are too tired to get dressed, let alone drive anywhere; when, if you get to the end of the day and your children have been fed, watered, and have clean nappies, then it counts as a good day. Everything boils down to the bare minimum to just get through the next hour.

My severe lack of sleep meant that I lost the ability to take joy in my children. Above all else, I knew I wanted that back. It took time and determination, but

I kept striving for that goal – for better and longer sleep for my kids and me, which would mean I had the energy and patience to really enjoy spending time with Alexandra and Harry again.

If you are reading this book, it could be that you are – as I was – in quite a dark place. Sleep deprivation can leave you at greater risk of depression; you are more likely to get ill as your immune system will be low, and when you do get ill, you may take longer to recover. It is draining, physically and mentally, and can damage your relationships with friends and family, and particularly your relationship with your partner. If you are working, it can affect your performance and impact on your ability to do your job properly. It is not easy to live with sleep deprivation day after day, week after week, month after month. So I want to make this promise to you – it will get better; there is light at the end of the tunnel. The tips and Trust Techniques in this book do work. Depending upon the Trust Technique that you decide is best for your family, it might take two weeks or it might take two months – but it will get better.

How to cope with sleep deprivation

There is only one cure for sleep deprivation – sleep! It is not the total amount of sleep that you get that counts – you might sleep for a total of twelve hours a night and still be sleep deprived. It is the broken and disturbed nature of the sleep you do get that is the problem. To get good sleep, you need to have long unbroken stretches of sleep where you get the benefit of non-REM sleep. It is especially important for the first three to four hours of sleep to be unbroken, as this is your core sleep. But if you have children, and especially a young baby, undisturbed sleep can be unrealistic, and this can have a huge impact on your coping mechanisms. It is not for nothing that sleep deprivation is used as a torture device! So how do you cope when there is little prospect of your getting that all-elusive full night's sleep?

- Sleep or rest whenever you can. Forget about the housework, cleaning, and ironing – they can all wait. When your little one is napping, you should be napping too.

111

- If possible, get some help from your partner, family, and friends. Most people understand how tiring looking after a baby can be and are more than happy to help out. Remember that the most important part of your sleep is your 'core sleep' which happens in the first three to four hours, so this is the sleep which you should be trying to protect. If you can, ask someone else to cover your little one's wakings during the start of the night. If you have a partner, think about swapping round every couple of nights, so you cover the night wakings that occur at the start of the night for two days and then your partner does the following two.

- If you feel up to it, try some gentle exercise. This will increase your stamina and strength, both of which will help you through those tiring nights and difficult days. Bundle your little one into her pram and go for a walk, or try yoga or pilates – there are some great DVDs and books out there, and your baby will love seeing you try out all those positions. In some areas, there are even classes for mums where you can take your little one with you.

- If possible, try to ensure you get some 'me' time each day. Even if it is only fifteen minutes a day, make sure you have some time where you focus on yourself as an adult rather than a parent. If possible, ask your partner or your parents to look after your baby while you have a nap, have a bath, go for a walk, meet up with friends, have a massage, or go to the cinema. If this isn't possible, try to make sure that you get some time to focus on yourself when your baby is in bed. Call a friend, read a book, watch a movie on the TV, and if you have the time and energy, try starting a new hobby (or continuing an old one).

- Remember that it will get better. It is hard to keep in mind when you are just trying to get through one exhausting day after another, but I promise things will get better. Use my

Twelve Top Tips in Chapter 3. Pick a Trust Technique from Chapter 4 that best suits your family and follow it every nap and bedtime. I promise that you will see a difference within a couple of weeks, and knowing that you are doing something – that you have a plan – to help your baby sleep better and for longer, makes it easier to deal with the tiredness.

- Know that you are not alone. The majority of parents will go through periods of their baby not sleeping. It is normal for babies to wake during the night – while you are up with your little one, remember that there are millions of babies all over the world, keeping their parents up too!

- It really does help to talk about it. Whether it's with your partner, family or friends, your doctor, paediatrician, or health visitor, try talking about what you are going through. The Internet is full of websites and forums for parents. For those in the UK, your health visitor is trained to help and your local Sure Start centre should have information on groups and play sessions where you can meet other families. Libraries are often good places to find out about local groups for parents. In the UK, the National Childbirth Trust (NCT) is a great charity with lots of information and many local branches that run several different groups and meet-ups for parents.

- If you find that you cannot sleep, even when you have the opportunity, it might be that you have become severely sleep deprived. I found I physically could not sleep when Alexandra and Harry were napping, and at night it would take me between two and three hours to fall asleep. I had severe sleep deprivation. If this sounds familiar, it is important that you see your doctor. There are medications that can help you to sleep, even if you are breastfeeding.

If you are a partner, family member, or friend of someone who is sleep deprived, there are things you can do to help. It can be a very difficult time for any parent who is sleep deprived and yet the one cure for it – a prolonged period of undisturbed nights – is often not a possibility. Sleep deprivation has knock-on effects on all aspects of a person's life. It affects their concentration, their ability to make decisions, their temperament, and their health. It leaves them at risk of depression and more susceptible to illness. It can put a huge strain on their relationships with partners, family, and friends. Someone suffering from sleep deprivation needs support from those around him or her. It will get better. There are no quick fixes, but the tips and Trust Techniques detailed in this book will help. In the meantime, try to ensure that the caregiver who has sleep deprivation is given as much opportunity to sleep as possible. If possible, take over the night shifts (even if this is only at weekends, it will make a difference), and especially try to cover wakings that occur at the start of the night. This protects the 'core' sleep that is so important. Let the person talk about what they are going through and discuss a plan of action – for example which of the twelve top tips you think would help and which Trust Technique you think would suit the family best. Let them have some 'me' time where they are not looking after the baby and can do something unrelated to parenthood. This opportunity to focus on themselves as an adult rather than as a parent can do wonders for their self-esteem and confidence.

Chapter 8: And Finally...

If you follow the tips in this book and are consistent in using your chosen Trust Technique, then very shortly your baby should start to sleep better and longer. You may find, however, that once your little one sleeps through, you don't. This is perfectly normal. You need to remember that you have been sleep trained to wake several times a night, and it will take you a few nights to adjust to sleeping undisturbed for longer. Make sure you give yourself a winding-down period before bed – take a bath, read a book, have sex – and know that it will get better. Our bodies do adjust quickly so it won't be long before you, like the rest of your family, will be having a peaceful night's sleep.

I wrote this book so that sleep-deprived parents had one single resource they could turn to if their baby was having sleep problems. I have sought to provide parents with alternatives to controlled crying – the five Trust Techniques that build on the bond of trust between parent and baby – as well as detailing the best tips for helping your little one to sleep. I particularly wanted this book to look at the effects a sleepless baby has on the whole household, and provide some strategies and ideas for those with other children in the family. Together these will provide you with the tools you need to help your baby learn good sleep habits, while minimising the impact on the rest of your family.

As your baby grows and develops, she will go through more stages of night-waking. Illness, teething, developmental leaps – all will probably mean your baby, and you, will have a few nights of disturbed sleep. It is important to follow your instincts as a parent when these occur: babies and children do sometimes need parental help in settling to sleep. But once they are past this stage, and if they once again have come to rely on you as their sleep-association device, you can use the Trust Techniques to help them remember how to settle happily on their own again. And this time, it shouldn't take as long.

Raising children is the hardest job there is, but it is also the most rewarding. I hope this book will enable parents to forget about the sleep deprivation and instead enjoy the wonder and joy that comes from watching their children grow up.

Further Resources

- Gerhardt, Sue (2004) *Why Love Matters: How Affection Shapes a Baby's Brain*, London: Routledge.

- Gonzáles, Carlos (2012) *Kiss Me! How to Raise Your Children with Love,* London: Pinter and Martin Ltd.

- Leach, Penelope (2010) *Your Baby and Child*, London: Dorling Kindersley.

- Millpond Sleep Clinic (2005) *Teach Your Child to Sleep: Solving Sleep Problems from Newborn Through Childhood,* London: Hamlyn.

- Pantley, Elizabeth (2002) *The No-Cry Sleep Solution: Gentle Ways to Help Your Baby Sleep Through the Night*, New York: McGraw-Hill.

- Sears, William (2007) *Night-time Parenting: How to get your Baby and Child to Sleep*, New York: Plume.

- Sears, William and Sears, Martha (2005) *The Baby Book: Everything you need to know about your baby from birth to age two*, New York: Harper Thorsons.